Grandmother
BY ANOTHER NAME

Grandmother
BY ANOTHER NAME

Carolyn J. Booth and Mindy B. Henderson

*Endearing stories about what we call
our grandmothers*

RUTLEDGE HILL PRESS®

NASHVILLE, TENNESSEE

Published by Rutledge Hill Press®, Inc., 211 Seventh Avenue North, Nashville, Tennessee 37219. Distributed in Canada by H. B. Fenn & Company, Ltd., 34 Nixon Road, Bolton, Ontario L7E 1W2. Distributed in Australia by The Five Mile Press Pty., Ltd., 22 Summit Rd., Noble Park, Victoria 3174. Distributed in New Zealand by Tandem Press, 2 Rugby Road, Birkenhead, Auckland 10. Distributed in the United Kingdom by Verulam Publishing, Ltd., 152a Park Street Lane, Park Street, St. Albans, Hertfordshire AL2 2AU.

Typography by Roger A. DeLiso, Nashville, Tennessee
Design by Harriette Bateman
Jacket photograph by Robert Pierce

Library of Congress Cataloging-in-Publication Data

Booth, Carolyn J., 1938–
    Grandmother by another name / Carolyn J. Booth and Mindy B. Henderson.
       p.   cm.
    ISBN 1-55853-481-4
    1. Grandmothers.   2. Nicknames.   3. Grandparenting.
I. Henderson, Mindy B., 1960–   . II. Title.
HQ759.9.B67   1997
306.874'5—dc21   97-5760
                                                                        CIP

Printed in the United States of America

3 4 5 6 7 8 9—01 00 99 98

Acknowledgments

Thanks to our husbands,
David and Mark,
and to Bryan Curtis, Amy Lyles Wilson, and Larry Stone
for believing in this book. Your help and encouragement made
our efforts possible, as well as fun!

My grandmother,
Sarah Mattie Viola Warren Jenkins
(mother of sixteen children and
grandmother of twenty-nine grandchildren),
and my granny,
Hilda Vance Holland Booth
(mother of two children and grandmother of four).
I miss you both very much.

Mindy

Introduction

*O*ne day my oldest daughter, Mindy, called and asked if I would meet her for lunch. That wasn't unusual, but as I sat down, she had a sly grin on her face as she handed me a little bag.

"What's this?" I asked.

"Just look inside," she answered, bubbling with excitement.

I opened the bag and found two comical coffee mugs: one for Grandpa and one for Grandma with pictures showing before, during, and after delivery. As I gazed at the mugs, many emotions flooded my mind and heart—surprise, happiness, excitement, but most of all, love for this daughter of mine. A baby? No way! Someone had moved the clock forward.

As I drove home, my mind started to race. "I'm going to be a grandmother! No, not me. That's my mother! What will I be called? Grandmother, Granny, Nana, Mi Mi?" I began to say the words out loud. They did not seem to fit me.

In the months that followed, almost daily someone would ask, "What do you want the baby to call you?"

When our grandson, Jared, was born, I began to call myself Grandmother to him. "Come to Grandmother," "Grandmother loves you," and on and on.

All three of my daughters call me Mom. They would say, "Mom, isn't he sweet?" or "Mom, let me hold him." Despite my "Grandmother" urging, Jared had something different in mind.

One day as I fed this adorable little boy, he had had quite enough. As I offered him one last bite, he looked at me and clearly said, "No, no, Mom Mom!"

I became Mom Mom that day. Now that is my name to all six of my grandchildren.

So this book is offered as inspiration for all grandmothers everywhere—old, young, young at heart, soon-to-be grandmothers, and in memory of those who live on in our hearts.

What do you want your grandbaby to call you?

Carolyn

Grandmother

BY ANOTHER NAME

GeeTee

For some odd reason, my daughter has always shortened her sentences with initials. For instance, SFSG stands for "so far so good" and LY means "love you." I could go on and on. When she was growing up, this practice used to drive me nuts. It kept me on my toes, however, as I would find myself standing in the house trying to figure out what in the world the last initials she had yelled to me stood for.

When my grandson was born, my daughter named me G.T., for Grandma Thomas (Thomas is my last name). I didn't like the initials, so I took it upon myself to change the spelling to GeeTee. Of course, my grandson began calling me GeeTee.

One day, when he was seven years old, I was reading to him from the Shel Silverstein book called *The Giving Tree*. The story is about how a tree gave all that she had to a young boy so that he could be happy. After we read the story, I noticed that my grandson sat pondering what he had just heard.

"GeeTee, you always keep me when my mom and dad need a babysitter, right?"

"Right," I said.

"And you sometimes pick me up from school, and come eat lunch with me, and talk to me when I have had a bad day, right?"

"Right," I again responded, wondering where in the world his little mind was going.

"Whatever I needed, you would do for me, wouldn't you?" he asked.

"You'd better believe it!" I answered.

"Well, in that case, GeeTee can mean that you are my giving tree. Just like the book, right?"

I swallowed hard. What is it in the minds of children that can pull at your heart when you least expect it?

"I would love for GeeTee to mean 'giving tree' if you want it to," I said to him.

"Then that's what it is!" he said.

Then he hugged me and ran off to play.

I cried. How special my grandson is to me!

Families will live on through
the stories we tell our children and grandchildren.

Bob

$\mathscr{T}$ have always called my grandmother Bob. Her real name is Hettie Bob, but everybody just calls her Bob. I'm not quite sure why her parents named her a man's name. I always felt a little strange about the fact that other kids had Grandmother or Grand-ma—and I had Bob.

My Bob is the best! She is so funny and full of herself. I get the biggest kick out of being around her. She has the greatest stories about my mother when she was little, and I love just sitting and talking to her. Having a man's name doesn't seem to bother her in the least. It makes her unique.

But let me tell you another unusual thing about her. Hettie Bob married a man named Eddie Cobb. So they are Hettie Bob and Eddie Cobb; she is Hettie Bob Cobb. I think for now, I'll stick to calling her Bob.

Dear Dear

$\mathcal{B}$e careful what you say around your grandchild! Whenever there was an accident, whether it was spilled milk or a cut on the finger, I would loudly exclaim, "Oh, dear, dear!" It didn't take long for my walking, full-of-life little granddaughter to catch on to this. Soon, each time something happened that she wanted to show me, I would hear her voice calling out, "Dear, dear!" and she would grab my finger and lead me to whatever interesting new discovery (or accident) she had made. Now I am Dear Dear to all of my grandchildren—which I find very endearing indeed!

I Love My Grandmother Because…

She gives me money.

As My Grandmother Always Says...

"If you eat too much candy, your teeth will fall out."

"Pretty is as pretty does."

"Chew with your mouth closed."

"You look just like your mother (father) when you do that!"

"Carrots make your eyes strong."

"You are Grandma's precious angel!"

"If your momma and daddy say no, you just call me!"

"Tell Grandma all about it."

"Come let me kiss it."

"You know no matter what, I love you!"

"What's the magic word?"

"Be sure to say your prayers."

Lolly

*L*olly—the name sounds like a sucker. And that's exactly what I am, a sucker for anything sweet coming from my grandchild.

Because this was my first grandchild, I searched for a name that would be different, but meaningful. When I met my husband thirty-six years ago, I was introduced to him as Lolly. I was given the name Lolly by my two-year-old brother who couldn't pronounce Lanell, my real name. My husband still occasionally calls me Lolly.

So, when my first grandchild came along, I undertook the awesome task of finding the perfect name. Grandma, Granny, Nanny—these all ran through my mind. I really liked the name that my parents were called by my children. Because my maiden name begins with a *B*, my children call my parents Mamma B and Daddy B. Unfortunately, my last name begins with a *P* and I didn't really want to be called Mamma P. Go figure!

That's when my husband had a brilliant idea. Our grandbaby would call me Lolly, my nickname. Of course, my husband is called Pop. Lolly, Pop—are we suckers for that child? You bet we are!

Grossmutter Grossie

*W*hen I was a little girl, my family took a trip from San Diego to Indiana every summer to visit my mother's family. The thing I remember most was visiting with my great-grandmother, Grossie. She was my mother's grandmother, and she helped raise my mom and her sister and brother. I remember distinctly arriving at Grossie's house and seeing this little old woman with hair as white as cotton (and just as soft) come out to greet us. She was always so interested in everything that we had to say! She would ask us questions about what interested us. We would try to rush through her questions however, because our favorite part of visiting Grossie was hearing all of her stories about when she was a young girl.

Grossie is short for *Grossmutter,* German for "grandmother." Grossie moved to the United States when she was very young. My favorite story concerns one of her very first jobs in the States, as a nanny at the age of fifteen. One day while she was out with her charges, a horse and carriage careened through the street and was going to hit Grossie and the children. She pushed the kids to safety and was trampled by the carriage. She was rushed to the doctor who told her mother that she would probably not live, and if she did, she wouldn't be able to have children. When she would tell me this story, it became so real I could see the horse and carriage coming and my Grossie saving the little ones. I would get the warmest feeling inside. The amazing thing about this story is that she did, in fact, live to be ninety-five years old! She was also the mother of two very healthy children.

In America, the word "gross" describes things that are less than appealing. To me, my Grossie was the sweetest living angel that God ever put on earth.

I Love My Grandmother Because…

We sit outside at night, look at the sky,
and talk about anything I want to talk about.

Midwest Mammy

*M*y mom, Kay, is affectionately referred to as Mammy by her three adoring granddaughters. Her husband, of course is called Pappy. The word "mammy" conjures up many images, but perhaps the predominant one is of a large, matronly lady from the South. But not this mammy! She is a petite, real-estate salesperson from the Midwest! Her golfing foursome cannot believe she allows herself to be called Mammy. "Kay," they insist, "you don't look or act like any mammy we have ever seen!"

But Kay's first grandchild is a southern girl, born and raised in Tennessee. Kay had carefully chosen the names Grammy and Grampy for the first grandchild to call her and her husband. Nevertheless, one day "Mammy" came out of the mouth of that babe, and it sounded so endearing that it stuck!

So now, as the ladies tee off each week at the country club in Illinois, there's a mammy in the group—a very proud midwestern version!

Step-Grand

*A*ll stepgrandmothers take note! Sometimes it is hard to enter into the family as a stepgrandmother, but this one is very special. Kelly calls her Step-Grand, because she is so very, very, very nice. She cooks good food, buys Kelly lots of presents, and as far as Kelly is concerned, is connected by blood.

I Love My Grandmother Because...

She always comes to my ball games. She pays me
one dollar for home runs!

Boo-Boo

Usually the first grandchild sets a precedent by naming the grandparents for all future grandchildren, but not in this case. The second-born child of our family, Kathy, was expected to call her grandmother Grandmother Shepherd, just as her older sister was already saying. But no, to this precocious child Grandmother Shepherd became Boo-Boo.

Why would a child choose BooBoo? Was it because her grandmother was always full of surprises, perhaps hiding and yelling "Boo," or because she could play a fun game of peekaboo? Was this child developing verbal skills around Halloween, being about ten months old at that time? The reasons seem endless.

One thing is sure though, Boo-Boo aptly fit Grandmother Shepherd, an extraordinary woman who embraced all of life, especially the surprises. And Kathy, in her ten-month-old wisdom, had pegged the perfect name for her!

Trixie

*H*er children and grandchildren called her Trixie. Our friends lovingly referred to her as Miss Trixie. My grandmother had a warm smile, a hearty laugh, and a quick wit. But it was her tricks for making every task easier that got her the name of Trixie. Whether playing a game, learning to bake, or memorizing Bible verses, my grandmother could find a shortcut. We referred to this as "Trixie's little bag of tricks." She used her love for cooking to make people feel special. Her friends and her children's friends were the recipients of her yummy cakes and rolls. I remember trying to make a cake with her one day. Watching her mix the batter would leave me wondering how they could taste so good. You soon realized that she had her own little bag of tricks, such as a "dash" of this or a "pinch" of that. I find myself using many of her tricks in my day-to-day life now. And whenever I do, her knowing smile enters my mind and brings joy to my heart.

Nano Beach

*N*ano Beach lives a long way from my home, but not far from a beach. Every summer she would take our family to the ocean. She loved it so much and knew how to make our time there special. She would help us build wonderful sandcastles. She always knew where to find the very best shells! She knew interesting places to go and great places to eat; she even knew fun things to do when it rained. Because of my association with my grandmother and her love of the beach, I gave her the name Nano Beach!

"A baby is God's opinion that life should go on."

—CARL SANDBERG

Ha-Ha

My mother had four children of her own, but the prospect of becoming a grandmother left her somewhat anxious. Whenever my mother was with her first grandchild, she would get right in her face and pretend to laugh: "ha-ha-ha!" She would get the result that she was looking for when my precious little daughter would look at her and smile. This happened at each and every visit. "Ha-ha-ha!"

When my daughter Brenda was nearing two years old, my mother came once again to visit. As she walked through the door, Brenda ran to her and screamed, "Ha-ha!" Laughing, my mother picked her up and the name just stuck! Everyone in the family called her "Ha-Ha," and she was very proud of the name.

It is ironic that my mother suffered depression many times during her life. But she is remembered as Ha-Ha, which always brings to mind the happy times that we shared with her.

She lets me sleep with her.

—

She lets me have a pacifier even though I'm too old.

—

She has a motorcycle.

—

She makes me feel important.

—

I like old things … and she is old!

—

She is a very funny honey!

Bylo

My son Larry was born during World War II. We lived in Maryland, and then moved to New Jersey. We were quite a long way from my parents, who lived in Tennessee.

After the war was over, we were finally able to make the trip down South to show off my new son! My parents were excited to meet their new grandson for the first time. My mother, Grace, would rock him and sing the song "Bylo Baby Bunting, Daddy's Gone A-Hunting" to him. This was a very special bonding for my son and his grandmother.

When we got home, Larry spoke of Bylo often. Thereafter, all of her grandchildren called her Bylo. Whenever I hear this song, I fondly remember my mother holding and rocking her new grandson, and the special happiness that we all shared.

Grand Micki

*T*his cool grandmother has a Volkswagen convertible named Minnie, a tattooed Minnie Mouse on her ankle, and the Disney store is an automatic stop on shopping trips with her grandchildren. Mickey Mouse is their favorite Disney character.

Micki is her name! Her grandchildren call her Grand Micki. She loves it and hopes they will remember her as a very fun and lovable character, just as they think of the well-known mouse!

I Love My Grandmother Because…

When I'm mad at my parents, I call her and she says, "Tell me what happened." We talk and I feel better.

Grand Gracie

*M*y birth name is Grace Elaine, but everyone calls me Elaine. My grandmother name came by way of my son-in-law, who decided he wanted his own special name for me. He started calling me Gracie. When our grandson was born, because he was living in another state, I would find myself telephoning just to hear him coo, make funny little chatter, or even just to cry! I wanted to know him and for him to know me, even though we were apart.

My voice soon became familiar to him as I would say, "Hi, David, I love you." My daughter would say, "David, it's Grand Gracie on the phone." For a while in all his chatter, I would catch the word "Acie." But then one day my phone rang, and I said, "Hello." On the other end of the line I heard, "Hi, Grand Gracie." I can't tell you how that made my day—or how I longed to give that child a grand hug.

GranNola

When Barrett, Nola's daughter, was in the sixth grade, one of her friends laughingly told Nola, "Someday, when you are a grandmother, you will probably be called GranNola."

Years later, she did become a grandmother; and yes, her granddaughter, Hannah, calls her GranNola! It always makes for quite a laugh in the grocery store. People are so confused when Hannah calls out, "GranNola!" Does that child urgently want a granola bar? No, she just wants something sweeter! She wants her grandmother, GranNola.

I Love My Grandmother Because…

It's a secret—but my grandma wears funny underwear.

Big Mama

When my first grandchild was just walking, he came into my house crying because he had fallen and gotten a "boo-boo."

"Come see Big Mama," I said to him. I picked that small, sweet child up in my arms. I kissed his hurt and dried those tears. I carried him back to my big rocking chair that had been handed down to me from my grandmother. He curled up in my lap. I sang to him and rocked him to sleep. I bet we rocked together, my grandson and I, for at least an hour.

To some, Big Mama would be an insult. But, to my small grandson, I *am* big. And to him, big means secure. So I am not insulted. Because there is nothing in the world finer than my grandchild cuddling in the security of my arms in that rocking chair.

Grandma Sunshine

*M*y daughter's family lives up North; my husband and I live in Florida. When my daughter and her family come to visit in the winter, my daughter always says, "We're going to see sunshine!"

Therefore, my grandchildren call me Grandma Sunshine. I take it as a great compliment because when they visit me I want them to feel warmth, happiness, and everything else that the word "sunshine" connotes.

I Love My Grandmother Because...

She understood when I was in love. She said, "Follow your heart! Go for it!" I'm happy I followed her advice.

Minner

$\mathcal{E}$very Sunday from the time my husband and I got married, we would go and eat Sunday lunch with my mother and dad. My mother's name is Mildred.

Therefore, every Sunday morning on our way to church, my husband would ask me, "Are we going to Mildred's for dinner?"

You know, you take your baby, you put her in the car, and you proceed to talk with your spouse about whatever you need to talk about. When your baby is under two, you don't really think she is picking up on what you say. Of course, I had an extremely bright first child (doesn't everybody?) who was listening to our every word and we didn't even know it.

One Sunday, when we got to my mother's to eat, my little girl looked at my mother and said, "Minner." We could not figure out why in the world she had called her grandmother that! We had always called her Grandmother Mildred to my daughter—and now it was Minner?

It wasn't until the next Sunday when we were in the car that my husband asked that same question: "Are we going to Mildred's for dinner?" "Bob," I said to my husband. "Mildred … dinner … Minner!" We got the biggest laugh out of the fact that our daughter had put the two together! Of course, after we explained it to my mother, she thought it was the most adorable name ever. And now, seven grandchildren later, she is Minner to the whole clan!

"If you see a book, a rocking chair, and a grandchild
in the same room, don't pass up a chance to read aloud.
Instill in your grandchild a love of reading.
It's one of the greatest gifts you can give."

—BARBARA BUSH

Mana

When I was growing up, I called my grandmother Mana. I wasn't really sure where she got the name, but it seemed to fit her so well. She was the perfect grandmother. Even though she had six grandchildren, whenever she was with you, one-on-one, she made you feel that you were the most special. She had a gift of listening without interruption to everything that was on your mind. She would respond to your questions with wisdom. She was happy, attentive, and loving. As I grew older, I wondered what the word "mana" meant. I looked it up in the dictionary. To some it was the miraculous food sent from the Lord to the Israelites on their journey to Canaan. To the Hawaiians it was a symbol of greatness: "the power of elemental forces of nature embodied in an object or person." It is also defined as one with "moral authority." Now, I don't know if she was given the name because my oldest cousin couldn't pronounce "Nana" or not. But how strangely wonderful that my Mana embodies all of the definitions of the word.

Grand Lady

One night when my daughter Karen was a teenager, she was having a slumber party. While the girls were upstairs, I was downstairs deeply engrossed in the movie of the week. I believe I remember Karen calling my name, but as we mothers do sometimes, I had tuned her out. Finally, a group of giggling teenage girls came and stood between me and my television set.

"Hey, lady!" my daughter said to me with a smile on her face, "can you order us some pizza?"

With that, all the girls giggled. From that minute on, Karen's friends called me Lady. My kids loved it and so did I!

When Karen was expecting my first grandbaby, one of my friends said, "Well, I guess now you will be called Grand Lady!" He was right! Now when any one of my four grandchildren calls out, "Hey, Grand Lady!" it warms my heart and takes me back to car pools, slumber parties, pizza, and giggling teenage girls.

BeBe

They call me a gushing grandmother. "Look at my sweet baby." "There's my baby." "Come see my baby." Those are phrases that make me sound like a broken tape recorder because I say them so much.

I guess I started this habit when my first grandchild was born. You know how you say things that you don't realize that you are saying? Well, I will never forget my grandchild, at the age of about fourteen months when he first began to talk, pointing his little finger at me and saying, "BeBe." My heart exploded! Now, not only was he my baby, but I was his.

I Love My Grandmother Because...

She says that there's no one like me! I am a masterpiece! I am special!

Oma

I was not yet forty when my daughter announced that I would soon be a grandmother. I still had two teenage sons! I could not be a grandmother yet! I was far too young!

As I was sharing my feelings of happiness but dread at the thought of being old with a friend of mine, she told me a story. My friend had moved to the United States from Germany when she was a teenager. She left all of her extended family behind, including her grandmother.

"We called her Oma," my German-born friend told me. "She was not your stereotypical grandmother. I remember watching her when I was young. She was so beautiful and full of life. She always had kind words when you were sad. She would always find the sun when there were clouds. Now I know she aged after we moved to the States, but to this day, I remember her dancing and smiling and always happy."

Twenty years later, my grandchildren call me Oma. I trust that they will remember me in the same way that my friend remembers her German grandmother.

Weez

When you think of a grandmother named Weez, you might picture an old woman in a rocking chair having just a little bit of trouble breathing. It may not be an appealing name to most, but to this young in spirit (and looks) grandmother, it was perfect. You see, her name is Louise, and her daughter-in-law called her by her name in front of the grandbaby. The baby then pronounced her name as Weez.

And do you know what? That grandbaby does take her breath away!

I Love My Grandmother Because…

She was strong, independent, and self-reliant. She lived until age ninety-seven. I'm a fourth-generation working mom!

Nannie Bird

My oldest daughter always called her grandmother Nannie. Nannie was one of those people who would talk and talk and talk. My daughter enjoyed listening to her grandmother. Just as girls do, they could sit and talk for hours.

Then my son came along, a boy of few words. He loved his grandmother, but the last thing in the world he wanted was to get engrossed in a long conversation with her. My husband and I would watch and smile as he tried to avoid getting into a "talk" with his Nannie.

One day, on the ride home from her house, my son announced to our family that Nannie talked so much she could talk to a bird! We told her that story and we all got such a laugh out of it that we started calling her Nannie Bird. By the way, she still tries to talk to my son—and he still tries to avoid it—thirty years later!

Olg

My grandmother lived through World War II. Both my father and my uncle fought in the war. For this reason, my grandmother was not real fond of the Germans at that time.

Now, my grandmother, Hilda, was a stout, rambunctious woman who did not put up with much from anyone. She had a very loud voice that carried far distances. Down deep, though she probably wouldn't want you to know it, she was a very sweet-natured woman who would do anything for you.

As a joke, because of her nature and because of her feelings about the war, my grandfather started calling her Olg. He said it was because she reminded him of the ladies over in Germany. My

Becoming a grandmother ranks right up there with
becoming a mother, only more fun and less work!

oldest cousin picked up on this and would tease her by calling her Olg. Pretty soon, we were all calling her that. I guess she finally accepted what she couldn't change.

Now, even though I wasn't born when World War II was being fought, every time I see a documentary on television or read something in the newspaper about it, I think of Olg and of how very much I miss her.

Top Ten Names for Grandmothers

1. Grandmother
2. Grandma
3. Granny
4. MawMaw
5. Nana
6. MiMi
7. Nannie
8. Me-Maw
9. Mama _____ (First or Last Name)
10. Grandmommy

Pow Pow

I have one granddaughter. When she was little, she called her grandfather (my husband) Paw Paw. We tried to teach her to call me "Grandmother," but the word was too difficult. Therefore, she went a long time without calling me anything.

One day, my daughter and I were discussing what I would be called. My granddaughter was sitting in the floor. She looked up during our conversation and called me Pow Pow! Of course, I just melted. I guess that solved our problem. I became Pow Pow that day.

Pow Pow could have come from her favorite toy that she carried around with her all the time. It was a little popcorn toy that would pop. I used to laugh with her about it and say "Pow pow, pow pow." Or it could be a derivative of Paw Paw. Whichever it is, I wouldn't trade my name for a million dollars.

She is now in second grade. She tells me that at school, the children tease her about Pow Pow, so she called me grandmother. But only at school. How special it is when she sees me away from her "friends," hugs my neck, and says "Hi, Pow Pow."

Around the Corner Nano

$\mathcal{M}$y grandmother lived, guess where? Around the corner. When my mother would go over to her house, she would yell to my dad, "I'm going around the corner!" "Where's momma?" I would ask. "She's at Nano's, around the corner," he would answer.

Soon, we all just referred to her as Around the Corner Nano. "Around the Corner Nano is having dinner for us tonight!", "Did you hear what Around the Corner Nano said today?" I've always been grateful for the fact that my grandmother and I were very close—just around the corner, in fact.

I Love My Grandmother Because…

She gives me what I need when I need it.
And today I need ice cream.

Mopsy

My daughter and I are blessed with blonde hair. Lots of blonde hair. Lots of curly, blonde hair. In fact, I am proud of the fact that there is no mistaking that Angela is my daughter. She looks just like me!

Of course, with the kind of hair that we have, we sometimes have difficulty getting it to look like we want it to. Not long after my first grandbaby was born, Angela was visiting. I was in the bathroom ranting and raving that I couldn't do anything with this mop of hair that I had. She teasingly called me Mopsy. Then she began to call my husband Popsy.

Guess what my grandbaby calls me now? And you know what? I love it! I figure that it's much better than Flopsy or Cottontail!

Groovy Grandmother (GG)

When my daughter told me that I was going to become a grandmother, I thought I was much too young. After all, I was only in my forties. I wore fashionable clothes, big earrings, high heels. I was teaching second graders, for heaven's sake. I was as far away from what my idea of a grandmother was as … well … suffice it to say that I was very far.

I truly agonized over this new experience. I had no idea what the baby would call me. My husband and I discussed it at great length. I was not sure I was ready for this.

Then the baby came. What a beautiful addition to my life! She was the sweetest thing I had ever seen.

Being ever so determined not to fit the stereotype of grandmother, on my first day back to teaching after the baby came, I entered that second-grade classroom in the coolest outfit I could find in my closet! As I walked through the door, one of the children shouted out, "Look! It's the groovy grandmother!"

I thought this was so cute I went home and told my husband. The next morning, as I opened my eyes, my handsome husband leaned over, sweetly kissed me, and said to me, "How is my groovy grandmother this morning?" At that moment, I knew that my world was complete. I had this wonderful man, a terrific son-in-law, a beautiful daughter, and a new grandbaby to help keep me young.

My name was Groovy Grandmother for a while, but soon after being blessed with three more grandchildren, they shortened my name to GG. Even so, they all know I'm still groovy!

I Love My Grandmother Because...

When I make a mistake, she always says,
"It'll be O.K. I still love you."

Dear Heart

My mother and I were always very close. She was at the hospital when I delivered her first grandchild. After everything was calm, she came in to spend a few minutes with me and her new granddaughter. We huddled close together and stared down at the baby. A rush of emotions flooded through her. She said that it didn't seem so long ago that she had held me just this way upon my birth.

"I want her to call me Dear Heart," she told me.

"Why, Mom?" I asked.

"Because she is the dearest thing to my heart," she replied.

She had other grandchildren after that and felt the exact same way about them. I remember her rocking them and saying, "You are just the dearest thing to my heart."

As the years passed, those children came to understand exactly what their grandmother felt—because they had that same kind of love for her.

Go-Go

When I was younger, I used to hear all of the kids at school talking about their grandmothers. "Grandmother got me this." "Grandmother said that." I didn't understand why I didn't have a grandmother.

Finally, one day, I went home very sad.

"What's wrong?" my mother asked me.

"Everybody has a grandmother except me," I choked out to my mother, trying to hold back the tears.

"Why, Marsha," my mom said. "Everybody has a grandmother, but not everybody has a Go-Go. You have a Go-Go!"

I had always called my grandmother Go-Go. My older cousin had given her that name. I didn't know she was my grandmother! I just knew that whenever I visited her home, we would go all kinds of different places, like to the store, or the park, or the library. She lived in California, and before we even got our bags unpacked, she would excitedly begin to tell us about all the things we were going to do and the places she had planned to go. I was always excited to go to Go-Go's house because I knew that she would have somewhere interesting and new to take me.

As I grew older and the kids talked about their grandmothers, instead of feeling left out and sad, I straightened my shoulders and thought to myself, "They may have a grandmother, but I have a Go-Go!" I was very proud.

I Love My Grandmother Because...

My grandma is in heaven,
but when I do something special, my mom says,
"I'm so proud of you and Grandma would be too."

Cuckoo Nana

I loved to go to my grandmother's house when I was little. We would play and laugh and have so much fun. She had a large cuckoo clock that fascinated me. My mother said that every time it would chime, I would run and watch the bird come out. My grandmother would stand beside me, and together we would announce with "cuckoos" whatever hour it was.

Because I loved the clock so much, whenever I would cry, my grandmother would do a funny face and say, "Cuckoo, Cuckoo," to cheer me up. That's why I call her Cuckoo Nana. She was so funny and always so happy! Now that old cuckoo clock stands in my house, and every time the clock chimes, I remember Cuckoo Nana and look forward to the day when I can hold my own grandchild in front of the clock and tell him or her about *my* grandmother, my Cuckoo Nana.

Gong Gong

My husband and I lived right down the street from my parents. My mother had her own sales business and was on the go all of the time.

As my daughter grew older, she got into the habit of running to our front window to watch for her grandmother's car to go by. Every morning, you could see her little body inside the curtain looking out the window. Pretty soon, I would hear my mother's car horn blowing and I would hear my daughter say, "Gone, gone."

Somehow, "Gone, gone" turned into Gong Gong, and that's a very appropriate name for a grandmother who's always on the run!

I Love My Grandmother Because...

She fixed a special room at her house just for me!

Mama Too

The oldest of five children, I was first to marry and first to present my parents with a grandchild. We lived close to my parents and we visited often. We all called my mother "Mama." I had a little brother just eight years old when my baby, Virginia, was born.

Whenever we would visit, Virginia would hear me, my three sisters, and her eight-year-old uncle call my mother Mama. One day, in her wide-eyed innocence, she went up to my mother and asked, "Are you my mama, too?"

"Yes I am!" she said. And from that moment on, she has been Mama Too to all ten of her grandchildren.

I Love My Grandmother Because...

She puts "magic cream" on my boo-boos
and makes the hurt go away.

Hester Heifer

I grew up in California, and my grandmother lived in rural Tennessee. I remember visiting her as a child. I was always amazed that instead of opening a can of green beans, she would pick them from her garden. When we had colds, she would make a "snuff paste" and put it all over our chests. She had a farm with many cows. Her lifestyle was quite different than the one that I had in California!

It was not uncommon to hear people call my Grandma Hester "bull-headed." She was so stubborn! She had her way, and, as people say, it was her way or the highway!

On one particular visit with Grandma Hester she and I discussed the "heifers" that she had on her farm. During this same visit, I got a cold. She, of course, made up her home "snuff" remedy and prepared to put it on my chest. Well, I did not want that stuff on my chest at all! She was telling me to be still and I was twisting and screaming until I finally called out, "You're just Hester Heifer!"

"What did you say?" she laughed.

Because I was so young, I didn't really understand the difference between a heifer and a bull—to me they were the same. All I knew was that she was so stubborn.

From that day on, I have called her Hester Heifer. Our family has had so many laughs with this. Now I have four children of my own. And do you know what everyone in my family tells me? That I am just as "bull-headed" (or "heifer-headed" as the case may be) as my grandmother. What a compliment! But I have news for them—there is no way my grandchildren will ever call me a heifer.

Just try me!

"He thinks I'm his grandma."

"His grandma?" Harvey kept his hand on the key but didn't turn it. "You're not, are you?"

Laurie, standing behind Mattie, shook her head back and forth.

"Oh, no, but he needs one," said Mattie.

I Love My Grandmother Because...

She makes rolls like heck!

—

She has great stuff in her attic.

—

She gave me my mom's doll.

—

She taught me to tie my shoes.

—

She says, "If you work hard, you can be anything you want to be!"

—

Her house always smells good!

MaNu

My granddaughter was my first grandchild. I was totally the gloating grandmother. I took her everywhere and would say to anyone I came in contact with "This is my new grandbaby!" Or, "Have you seen my new baby? Isn't she precious?"

As she approached thirteen months, we would sit on the floor and play. I would tease her and say, "This is my new toy" and she would imitate me and say "No, my new toy." It is no wonder that soon after when she needed anything she would yell out "MaNu!"

When your first grandchild is born, it is like getting the most wonderful present that you could ever dream of. And the older the child gets, the more wonderful it gets. She may not be "my new" grandbaby anymore in the sense of time—but every day brings new adventures and experiences. For that reason, she will always be my new grandbaby and I will always be her MaNu.

Lady Di

*M*y mother is very beautiful. About the time of my son's birth, she and my father were getting divorced. It was an extremely difficult time for my mother because not only was she going through this marital change, but she was also about to become a grandmother for the first time.

One day, she and a friend of hers were looking through a magazine.

"That's a cute haircut, Diane," my mom's friend said to her, pointing at a picture of Princess Diana.

The next time we saw my mom, she had a new haircut and looked a lot like Princess Diana! My husband started calling my mother Lady Di. My son has picked this up and that's what she is called. To my son and me, she *is* royalty.

Rice Grandma

*R*ice Grandma received her name and distinction due to her specialty—rice pudding. This was more than ordinary cafeteria rice pudding, this was "Rice Grandma Rice."

Everyone was expected to stop by Rice Grandma's after church on Sunday. Rice Grandma would greet us in her "uniform," a calico apron that covered her dress from top to bottom and high-button (actually laced!) shoes. Sitting down to a meal at Rice Grandma's meant two things, egg bread buns and Rice Grandma Rice, the texture and consistency of which was unmatched (and is sorely missed). Rice Grandma always made rice because it was something that her small grandchildren could eat. The food fest at Rice Grandma's house continued until you walked out the door, and a bag of egg bread buns always accompanied you home.

When Rice Grandma was ninety, she finally got a new stove. It was time, she decided. She was a tiny, feisty woman who was full of herself. She died when I was eleven years old. Hers was the first funeral I ever attended. All of my relatives were there and it felt like just another family gathering—except one thing was missing. Rice Grandma was not in the kitchen. When I finally worked up the nerve to view Rice Grandma's body, I knew that aspect of my childhood was over—there she was with her high shoes and neat hair—but the key thing that I remember was that it was the first time I had ever seen her without her apron.

At that moment I thought that I would never eat Rice Grandma Rice out of respect to her. I have since relented, but it has never tasted the same. I think it is because her secret ingredients of love

I Love My Grandmother Because…

She tells me funny stories about my daddy when he was my age.

and care are not mixed in, but I can't prove it. Here is the recipe that I would like to share so that maybe you can create these wonderful memories for your grandchild.

Rice Grandma Rice

½ cup rice (not instant)

Dash salt

1 cup water

2¼ cups milk

½ cup sugar

Cinnamon

*C*ook rice, with salt, until water is absorbed. Add milk, and cook over double boiler until milk is absorbed. Add sugar. Sprinkle with cinnamon. Serve warm. (But it's good cold, too!)

Woppy

$\mathcal{M}$y husband, a baseball coach, is called Poppy by the grandchildren.

Our grandson learned to play ball as soon as he could hold a ball and a small bat. We got a thrill out of playing with him, and we would give him cheers and claps of encouragement. One day, in my excitement at seeing him hit a ball, I said, "You really wopped that ball." My son-in-law picked up on that and jokingly began calling me Woppy—which went very well with Poppy.

Our grandchildren all play school sports now and at baseball games they know that Woppy and Poppy are there cheering for them to "wop that ball!" And I'm proud to say they usually do!

Children's children are a crown to the aged.

—Proverbs 17:6

Ma'am

$\mathcal{I}$ wanted to be called Gram by my grandchildren. I also wanted my grandchildren to have nice manners. For this reason, I think I thoroughly confused their little minds.

When I would call them and they would say, "Huh?" or "What?" I would say, "Ma'am" or "Yes, ma'am."

"Do you want a sandwich?"

"No."

"No what?"

"No ma'am."

"Good."

Pretty soon, my granddaughter would run into my kitchen and say, "Ma'am, milk." So now Gram has changed to Ma'am and I am the well-mannered grandmother. Thank you very much!

Ease

*M*y first grandson named me Ease. It, of course, is short for Louise.

I had a hard time believing that I was going to be a grandmother. It was difficult to think that I was old enough. And harder still to believe that I was wise enough—as wise as grandmothers are supposed to be. I felt that the transition from mother to grandmother would be a difficult one.

But when my grandson called me Ease for the first time, I knew that everything I had conjured up about my shortcomings were wrong. I actually made the transition with "ease." Do you know why? Because that grandson of mine is so "easy" to love! And when everything is said and done—love is all you really need anyway, right?

Oh me

I am the mother of four girls. When my oldest daughter, Lisa, had our first grandbaby, Rachel, I was the truly doting grandmother.

You know how you have phrases that you don't realize that you use? Well, mine happened to be "Oh Me." Each time Rachel would give me a hug it was "Oh me, you are so sweet!" When she would smile, I would say "Oh me! You are so cute!" Even dirty diapers would arouse an "Oh me!" So when it came time to call out for me, she cried, "Oh me!" How sweet that name rings in my ears!

Timothy learned about God from his mother and grandmother when he was a small boy.

—2 TIMOTHY 1:5

Andmomma

$\mathcal{M}$y grandchild was going to call me Grandmomma, the name I had chosen. We were all sitting around the den one night playing the game of "Point, who's that?" with him. He was delighted to be the center of attention.

"Who's that?" We pointed to my son-in-law. "Daddy," he said.

"Who's that?" My daughter was next. "Momma," he answered, proud to be getting them all correct so far.

"Who's that?" My husband. "Anddaddy." He ran and patted my husband's knee.

"Who's this?" I pointed to myself. "Andmomma." He jumped up in my arms.

"Good boy!" we all encouraged.

That night in bed, my husband said to me, "This is just how it's supposed to be, isn't it?"

"What?" I asked.

"I hope he always thinks of us as extensions of his momma and daddy. I love the names Anddaddy and Andmomma."

I snuggled up close to Anddaddy and thought, "So do I."

Ten Famous People Influenced by Their Grandmothers

1. **Maya Angelou**—African-American poet whose autobiographies include many stories told her by her grandmother.

2. **Hans Christian Andersen**—nineteenth-century Danish author whose grandmother told him folktales that he included in his stories.

3. **Alex Haley**—African-American author whose greatest success, *Roots,* was born of the genealogical history recited by his grandmother.

4. **Langston Hughes**—poet, writer, and preeminent interpreter of the African-American experience, who was raised by his grandmother.

5. **Sir Walter Scott**—often considered the inventor of the historical novel, his grandmother entertained him as a child with stories of their ancestral Scottish border country.

Ten Famous People Influenced
by Their Grandmothers

6. **Eleanor Roosevelt**—wife of President Franklin D. Roosevelt and activist for the poor, youth, and minorities who was raised by her grandmother.

7. **James Madison**—fourth president of the United States, who was tutored until age eleven by his grandmother, Frances Madison.

8. **Sir Isaac Newton**—English scientist, astronomer, and mathematician, described as "one of the greatest names in the history of human thought," who was raised by his grandmother from age three to eleven.

9. **Alexander I**—Czar of Russia (1801–25), who was taken at birth by his grandmother to supervise his preparation to assume the throne.

10. **Hiawatha**—fictional Ojibwa hero of a poem by Henry Wadsworth Longfellow, who was raised by Nokomis, his wrinkled and wise grandmother, "daughter of the Moon."

Honey

*W*hile vacationing in Hawaii, I found myself at the pool one day, surrounded by children playing and swimming. I kept hearing them say, "Honey, watch this!" and "Look, Honey!" At some point, I looked over to see who this Honey was that these children obviously adored. There, sitting by the pool, was their sweet, white-haired grandmother, laughing with them and clapping for their every talent!

Now that I am a grandmother, I'm teaching my grandbaby to call me Honey. I can't wait until she gets old enough to show off for me!

I Love My Grandmother Because…

She will read me my favorite story over and over and over again.

MeMoney

My daughter and her husband, who got married before my son-in-law went to graduate school, were struggling financially.

Therefore, each time as they left after visiting us, I would slide some money to my daughter.

"You don't have to give me money," she would always say, hugging me and slipping the money in her pocket. "But thank you; it really helps."

My daughter told me that sometimes she and her husband, as they would drive home, would say things like, "That is sweet for Mom to give me money" or "I wish Mom didn't feel like she had to give me money." And my grandson would be sitting in his car seat in the back, listening to each word.

One day, as my daughter was about to leave, my grandson ran into the kitchen and grabbed my leg. "MeMoney, MeMoney," he said.

Now, I save all of my quarters, dimes, nickels, and pennies for that sweet little thing. And he calls me MeMoney, a name that is priceless to me.

Bye-bye

*M*y grandmother is hilarious. I don't remember when I was just learning to speak, but my mom has told me that my grandmother wanted to teach me to say "Bye-bye." So she would get in my face, wave, and repeat, "Bye-bye, bye-bye." It didn't matter if we had just arrived at her house, it was the middle of the visit, or we were leaving, it was time for "Bye-bye, bye-bye."

Soon this became a huge joke between my mother and my grandmother.

"What do you want her to call you?" my mother asked my grandmother one day.

"The first thing that comes out of her mouth will be my name," my grandmother responded.

With all the bye-byes that my grandmother said to me, it is no surprise that one day when I was about ten months old, I looked at her and repeated, "Bye-bye, bye-bye." "Well, I guess my name will be Bye-bye," said my grandmother.

I have the fondest memories of getting to my grandmother's house and yelling "Hi-hi Bye-bye!" And of course, upon leaving, "Bye-bye, Bye-bye." I'd venture to say that I have the best Bye-bye in the world!

To-Ra

*A*s a good Irish Catholic, Christine loved everything Irish, so she insisted that her first granddaughter be named Shannon. Shannon's mother, Christy, wanted her to call Christine Monny-Mom, which she had called her grandmother. Monny-Mom was apparently a variation of Mommy's Mom, and Christy always talked to Shannon about Christine as Monny-Mom.

From the time Shannon came home from the hospital, Christine would sit and rock her and sing "too-ra-loo-ra-loo-ral" to her. It is the Irish lullaby that has the singer remembering her mother singing it many years ago and willing to "give the world if she could sing that song to me today."

Shannon's first word to her grandmother, when she was nine months old and walking in the door to visit, was "To-Ra." She called her To-Ra ever after, as did other grandchildren and great-grandchildren. Even Christine's husband and children often referred to her as To-Ra, and the engraving on her tombstone includes that name—To-Ra.

Over in Killarney
Many years ago
Me mother sang a song to me
In words so soft and low

A simple little ditty, in her
sweet old fashioned way.
I would give the world to hear
her sing this song today.

Too-ra-loo-ra-loo-ral
Too-ra-loo-ra-li
Too-ra-loo-ra-loo-ral
Hush now don't you cry.

Too-ra-loo-ra-loo-ral
Too-ra-loo-ra-li
Too-ra-loo-ra-loo-ral
That's an Irish lullaby.

Honey Graham

*P*atsy called herself Gram when talking to her first grandchild, Cody. "This is my baby," she would say. "This is my little honey," she would coo as she cuddled the infant close to her.

When Cody was one year old, he was vacationing with Gram in Florida. As she went to pick him up, he pointed at her with great excitement and said, "My Patsy!"

"No, Cody, I'm your Gram," she replied, pointing to herself.

"My Honey Graham," he announced with self-assurance and ownership.

The name said it all! A bond was sealed that day on the beach, and thereafter Patsy was called Honey Graham.

By the way, if you see a car with the license plate "Honey Graham," you'll know who is behind the wheel. The proud grandmother of Cody!

Marf

$\mathcal{K}$elsey was my mother's first grandchild and, as a result, had the dubious honor of determining the name that she and the future grandchildren would use to refer to my mother. Grandmother seemed too formal, and my mother refused to answer to some of its more common versions because she felt they were synonymous with old age—at least they made her feel old.

The family had always referred to my mother by her first name, Marge. When Kelsey was about eighteen months old and really beginning to speak, she attempted, as children frequently do, to imitate her parents. The problem was that Kelsey had a lot of trouble with her g sound, so Marge became "Marf." The name stuck, and my mother is now affectionately called Marf by her friends and family. In fact, she even has address labels that refer just to Marf.

Mu Mu

*W*hen she tried to say Mama, the baby's words came out as MuMu. The name stuck with this loving grandmother, who was an extraordinary woman. MuMu raised six children and raised them on her own. She was described by her granddaughter as "an angel on earth, a ray of sunlight when she entered the room. Someone that you loved to sit on the porch swing and talk with for hours." She was the ultimate grandmother in her grandchildren's eyes.

I Love My Grandmother Because…

She always says, "Tell the truth—God knows!"

Foreign Names for Grandmother

Chinese (father's mother): jou mouh
(mother's mother): ngoih jou mouh
French (grandma): grand-maman
(grandmother): grand-mère
German (grandma): Grossmama, Oma
(grandmother): Grossmutter
Greek: yaya
Italian: nonna
Japanese: solo, obachan
Korean: halmoni
Latin: avia
Mandarin Chinese (father's mother): zu mu
(mother's mother): wai zu mu
Norwegian (father's mother): farmor
(mother's mother): mormor
(either father's or mother's mother): bestemor
Polish: babka
Portuguese: avozinha
Serbo-Croatian (grandma): baka
(grandmother): baba
Spanish (grandma): yaya, abuelita
(grandmother): abuela
Swedish (father's mother): farmor
(mother's mother): mormor
Yiddish: bobe, bube, bubie

E-I-O

When Marcilee's grandbaby came to visit, she would sing "Old MacDonald" to him. She sang the words and let the baby do the "E-I-E-I-O." This was their very own special song. Each time the baby and his mother drove by where Marcilee worked, the baby would point and say, "E-I-O!" From that, he began to call her E-I-O and has done so ever since!

I Love My Grandmother Because...

She doesn't make me take naps if I don't want to, and she lets me do whatever I want—like lay in the grass and get itchy!

Minnie

*M*ary Ann was a lady of small stature, but the most distinctive quality about her was her voice. She had a small, squeaky voice. In fact, she sounded just like Minnie Mouse!

One day, her oldest grandchild noticed this while watching cartoons. "You sound like Minnie, Grandma!" And from that day on, all the kids called her Minnie.

I Love My Grandmother Because…

We have family hugs with her and PawPaw.

Hazelnut

At first, we were a little afraid of our grandmother. My first remembrance of her is when she was in her seventies. She lived in a big Victorian house in a small mining town in Kentucky. There was a Revolutionary War soldier's grave in her yard, and sometimes we would hear the doors rattle in her attic, so we were pretty much convinced that her house was haunted. She stood five feet tall and had a hunchback. Every time we went to her house, she fixed green pea soup and made us eat it all. My cousins lived with her and the main thing I remember them telling me is that she "shore could give some whuppins." As little boys, we thought she was crazy. Her name was Hazel, so we called her "Hazelnut"— but we never did it to her face!

IBO

In my husband's very small hometown, whenever you made a phone call, you would pick up the receiver and ask the operator to connect you to the number. When my husband's sister, Susan, was a little girl, she called her grandmother Ibo. This was short for Isabelle, which Susan could not pronounce.

Well, word must have traveled about Ibo's name. One day when Susan was still too young to use the phone, she picked it up and the operator asked her for the number.

"I want to talk to Ibo," Susan replied. As luck would have it, the operator knew just whom she was talking about and put the call right through! How surprised was Ibo when she heard her young granddaughter's voice on the other line. And how we all wish we could call her now.

I Love My Grandmother Because…

She can take her teeth out.

—

She tells me I am perfect.

—

When we play checkers, I always win! She's not a very good player.

—

She always cooks my favorite food!

—

She charges my four-wheeler.

—

She tucks me in.

BaBa

When I was a little girl, my grandmother often took me out to a farm where there were a lot of animals. There was a sheep that would always bleat at me. I am told that when the sheep would do this, I would giggle and run to my grandmother.

Whenever I wanted to go see the animals, I would look at my grandmother and say, "baa-baa." She adopted the name "BaBa" from me. Now, whenever I take my kids to a farm, I fondly remember the fun times in the farmyard with my BaBa.

I Love My Grandmother Because…

She makes great grilled cheese sandwiches.

Bink

When my first granddaughter was born, my daughter Debbie decided that she should call me by my first name, Sue. Sara, my granddaughter, had a hard time saying her *s*'s. One day, I stopped by to visit them on my lunch hour from work. As I was about to leave, Debbie said, "Sara, tell Sue good-bye!" Sara didn't respond.

"Sara, tell Sue good-bye," Debbie said once again. "She has to go back to work at the bank."

Sara still did not respond. But as I neared the bottom of the steps to leave, she ran up behind me and said, "Bye-bye, Bink."

You know, I handle money every day at the bank. And to some people that is where they store their treasures. But not for me. Mine is in the three adorable grandchildren who call me Bink.

Narc Nana

When I was in high school, the way we identified the tattle-tales in our class was by using the word "narc." "Watch out, she'll narc on you," we would say.

Every winter my grandmother would come to live with us. The first time she came, we were all very excited. It didn't take us long, however, to figure out that when we would do something wrong or tell her something private, mysteriously our parents would always find out. She told on us!

At the time I didn't think that was very cool of her. As winter would approach, all of my friends at school would say, "When's Narc Nana coming to town?" or "How long is Narc Nana going to stay?"

Looking back on it now that I am a parent, I know that she always told on us because it was in our best interest. But then, if we ever wanted to do something we shouldn't, we had three people to keep it from—Mom, Dad, and Narc Nana!

NaNa

*E*ach Friday after work, I would pick up one of our small grandchildren to spend the night at our home. For the ten-mile drive, I would put them in their car seat, adjust the rearview mirror so I could see them, and proceed to say words for them to repeat. One day as I was saying "Grandmama" to my granddaughter, she repeated, "NaNa." It blessed my heart and I have been NaNa to Christie and Will ever since.

I Love My Grandmother Because…

She gives good hugs.

Gandma

My mother wanted my baby to call her Grandmother. I explained that Grandmother was too long and I thought he should call her Grandma. He tried to pronounce it but couldn't say the *r*. So he calls her Gandma.

The strange thing about this, however, is that when I was little, I couldn't say my *r*'s either. I called my grandmother Gandmommy. She died before my son was born. I think it is interesting that my son and I chose such similar names for each of our "gandmothers" when we were young.

I Love My Grandmother Because…

She taught me about God. I always sat by her at church.

Grand Buddy

*H*er first child tried really hard to say Mother, but it always came out Muddy. Soon everyone called her Muddy. As her girls grew up, they realized that not only was she their mother, but she was their buddy, so they changed Muddy to Buddy. Her first grandchild, therefore, called her "Grand Buddy." There is a song entitled "My Buddy" that is a favorite of theirs:

Nights are long since you went away,
I think about you all through the day,
My Buddy.
I miss your smile, the touch of your hand,
I long to know that you understand,
My Buddy.

Buddy is in her nineties and lives in a nursing home away from her children and grandchildren, but they come to visit her often and have a very special place in their hearts for their grandmother, their cherished friend—their Buddy and Grand Buddy.

D.G.—Double Granny

I married young and quickly became the mother of a son. My husband and I were soon divorced, and I became a single, very young mother.

Just because I was a mother didn't mean that I gave up the things that I loved to do: riding a Harley, wearing leather, and staying young at heart.

You can imagine my surprise when my son told me that he and his wife were going to become parents. I was too young—way too young—to be the *G* word. I told everyone at the hair salon where I worked that I refused to be called Granny. Therefore, to kid me, every time I walked into work, they called out, "Here comes Granny!"

I had barely recovered from the shock that I was going to be a grandmother, when my son and daughter-in-law once again surprised me that I was going to be the grandmother not to one child, but to two! They were having twins! It was a double whammy—I was going to be a double granny.

The next day at work, everybody yelled when I came in, "Here comes Double Granny!" Well, I outsmarted them all. I taught my adorable little grandson and granddaughter to call me "D.G." They are sixteen months old now, and when they see me, they come running and calling out, "D.G.! D.G.!" This melts my heart. D.G. suits me just fine. Everyone knows what the letters mean, but it's kind of like that saying, "You can call me G., or you can call me D.G., but whatever you do, please don't call me Granny!"

I Love My Grandmother Because...

She taught me to make a garden.

Boat Grandma

When my brother and I were young, our father's business transferred him all over the world. Visits with our grandmothers were a rare treat, requiring travel over a long distance and a stay of several nights.

You know how it is when you sleep in a different house, in a different bed. You hear every little noise, every creak and pop. One of our grandmothers lived on an island on the St. Clair River in Michigan. At night, the huge lake and ocean freighters would signal, especially in the fog. It didn't take two young boys long to recognize those special night sounds as comforting noises that made us feel safe because we were at Boat Grandma's house.

We are now twenty-two and twenty-eight years old. Whenever we hear those special night sounds, they rekindle warm memories of our youthful visits to our Boat Grandma—who just turned eighty-nine!

My very favorite naming story is about Ed and Ethel, who were called the Jewish names "Zaide" and "Bubbie" by their grandson Josh.

When Josh went to nursery school, he talked continually about his zaide and bubbie. He told of adventures with them, and when show and tell day came, he announced that he would bring in his bubbie and zaide.

When he walked in with Ed and Ethel, his nursery school teacher said, "Who are these people?"

"Bubbie and Zaide," he said proudly.

"But … but," she stammered, "I thought they were gerbils."

—Lois Wyse, *Funny, You Don't Look Like a Grandmother*
(New York: Crown Publishing Group, 1988)

Other Mother

I agonized and fretted over what my grandbaby would call me. Like many other grandmothers, I felt I was much too young to be Granny or Grandma. For months after she was born, I just didn't call myself anything to her. Finally one day, she said to me, "Other mother." I thought to myself, "What a smart grandchild! She recognized that she not only has one mother, but also has me—her other mother!"

I Love My Grandmother Because…

She let me braid her hair.

Touter (pronounced Tutter)

My mother-in-law had a younger sister who could not pronounce sister, so she always called her Touter. As they grew older, they shortened her name to Tout.

Tout is like my other mother. She lives in the same town with us. Whenever I have a dinner party, she is always there to help out. She will make food and bring it. She will advise me as to what I should have. I think she is the finest mother-in-law and grandmother the world has ever known.

Now, Tout has a knack for using all the sayings that grandmothers are known for. Therefore, whenever we are sitting around and someone uses a quote—such as "Pretty is as pretty does," or "When you're finished eating, don't dance around the dinner table," we all laugh and say, "There's another Toutism!" My children pick up on this. I know that as they get older and these sayings are used in their presence, it will bring to mind their sweet Tout and how very much she means to all of us.

Moms

My grandmother, Moms, was a woman ahead of her time. She had lost her own mother to cancer when she was just five years old, so she grew up to be very independent. After my father was born, she was divorced and had to work to support my dad and herself. She continued to work even after she remarried, which was unusual for a woman in the 1950s.

When she became a grandmother, she felt she was still too young to be called Granny, so she chose the name Moms for herself. My childhood memories of Moms include going to movies, visiting her office, and eating the most fantastic Christmas Eve dinner every year, consisting of all of my favorite foods.

I always believed that Moms was a special person, but I realized what a true fan I had when I decided one summer to move three thousand miles away to see if things would work out with the man I loved. All of my friends and other family members thought I was crazy. Moms, on the other hand, told me a story about how she packed everything that she owned into a car and moved two

hundred miles away to marry her second husband and true love. I went with her blessing and support. Now I'm married to this wonderful man and we have two precious children. My family and I have since returned and now live less than a mile from this very special eighty-four-year-old grandmother and now great-grandmother, Moms.

Other Grandmother Names

BeBau
Big Bertha
Cookie
Coxie
DaMa
De De
Dear
Dear Dear
DoDa
DoDi
DoDo
Dot Dot
Dramma
GG Mama
GiGi
Goggi
Gram
Gramio
Grammy
Gran Gran

Grand Ma Ma
Grandie
Grandmole
Grandmom
GrandNanny
GrannyMama
Hoppy
Lu Lu
Mabe
Ma'dear
Mai Mai
MaMa
MaMia
MaMoo
MeMama
MeMommy
Mil
Mine
Mom Nee
Momma Maw

Mom O
Momo
Money Moms
Muner
Muz
Myrner
NaNelle
Nanee
Nanu
Neina
Nina
Noisy
Page
Po
Poppy
Queenie
Sue Sue
Sweet Pea
ToTo

Mammy

*M*y grandmother was the midwife in our small town. She delivered all the children in the town, including her own grandchildren. Everybody called her Mammy. I didn't even know she was my grandmother until I was older, and then I thought she must be related to everyone in the town. How very fortunate I was to have had her as my very own Mammy.

I Love My Grandmother Because...

She spoils me rotten.

Mama Bear

She was the divorced mother of two little boys. Then she married a man with a young son, who heard her two boys calling her Mama, and he tried to do the same. But this made his real mama mad.

So she tried to explain to him that he already had a mama, and she was his stepmama. One day she was frustrated in trying to explain this to him as he was looking at her collection of dolls and teddy bears, which he loved. "O.K.," he smiled at her and said, "then you are my mama bear!"

This name thrilled her friends. Before she remarried, she had been a petite 105 pounds, but with her new marital bliss, she had gained up to 165 pounds. "I do look like a mama bear!" she laughed.

Now all three boys are older and they have children of their own. Mama Bear is back down to her small size, has long blonde hair, and looks not a day over thirty. But she is still Mama Bear to her children and grandchildren—a very beautiful Mama Bear, indeed.

Chock

When my daughter Kimberly was little, she struggled to come up with a way to distinguish her grandmothers from one another. It just so happened that one of her grandmothers had dark-colored skin. Kimberly began to call her "my chocolate grandmother." Soon she shortened this, and to this day she calls her Chock, a name she is very proud of. And she's just as sweet as chocolate, too.

I Love My Grandmother Because…

She helps me with my homework and she knows all about math!

Pretty

When my grandson was eighteen months old, our family took a vacation to the beach. During this time off, I didn't take time to put my make-up on or fix my hair! Why would I? I was on vacation.

So, when we were outside I would say things like "Don't I look pretty today?" and "Doesn't my hair look pretty today?" My family chimed in with my joking and would say, "Mom, your legs look so pretty!" Or "Man, Mom, you are looking really pretty today!" Afterwards, they all started calling me Pretty.

My grandson picked this up and now he calls me Pretty. The neat thing about it is that a lot of people call me that now. It really boosts your self-esteem when you're walking through the mall and someone you know yells "Hey, Pretty!" I guess I could've chosen "Beautiful," but why push it?

Bon Bon

*H*ave you ever heard of the mythical woman who "just sits around eating bon-bons all day," intimating that she is pampered and lazy? That is not the case with this pretty, smart, working grandmother. Her name is Bonnie and her granddaughter calls her Bon Bon. The only thing that she has in common with her grandmother name is that she is every bit as sweet as the candy.

I Love My Grandmother Because…

She always let me rummage through her jewelry box.

Lottie Bad

Once when I was a little girl, I was at my Grandmother Lottie's house. She was sitting and talking to the other adults in the room. As she talked, she struck a match, lit a cigarette, and shook the match out. Like most children, I was attracted to the match. I walked over and grabbed the end of the match. As soon as I touched it, I burned myself. Lottie and the other adults were so involved in their conversation that they didn't see me touch it until after it was over.

I began crying and Lottie reached to comfort me. "Lottie Bad!" I cried. She picked me up, kissed my boo-boo, and took me to run some water over it. Of course, all of the other adults in the room picked up on Lottie Bad, and she has since been called that by us.

But the truth is, Lottie Bad should really be called Lottie Good. She is a wonderful grandmother, and aside from that incident, she has done a "lotta good" by me!

Mai Nie

*S*peaking of confusing! Hannah, Judy's granddaughter, heard Judy called many different names. Her son called her Mammy, her husband called her Granny, and she called herself Grammy. So, little Hannah just came up with her own grandmother name: Mai Nie. A combination of all the best names!

I Love My Grandmother Because…

She sang old songs like "Froggie went a-courtin'."
I wish I had a recording of her singing.

BeBack

*W*e all remember the touching scene in the movie *E.T.* where E.T. tells Elliott, "I'll be right here." Well, this story is much the same.

The child was the youngest of eight grandchildren. Because he was the youngest, he was very special to his grandmother. When she would visit, she paid close attention to him. They played, read books, and cuddled. As she would leave each time, he would cry and reach out to go with her. "Don't worry! I'll be back," she would say, hating to leave.

One day, as she was about to leave, he came up to her with his arms outstretched, and she picked him up. With his arms tight around her neck, through his tears, his voice quivered, "BeBack. BeBack."

To this day, he is the only grandchild who calls her BeBack. He is an adult now, but is confident that she will always "BeBack" and there is no need to worry.

JoMama

My name is Joanne, and my son laughingly said he was going to have my future grandbaby call me JoMama. "That way, when you're with him, somebody will call out to him, 'Is that Yo Mama?' and he'll say 'No, that's my JoMama.' " My son thought this was so, so funny.

Of course, being the jokester that he always has been, my son began calling me JoMama to the baby as soon as she was born. And you know what I've found? It is pretty funny!

I Love My Grandmother Because...

She is so wonderful, a flower is named for her, the Edna Earl daffodil!

I Love My Grandmother Because…

She sends me cards with gum and money.

—

She lets me fix her hair however I want to!

—

She has a whole room full of junk food and candy.

—

She says, "You are so pretty, you look just like your mommy."

—

She says, "If you need me, I'm just a phone call away."

—

She is a pretty nice lady.

—

She feeds me very well.

Bunny

When my son Jud was younger, he loved to come up to me, grab me around the waist, and compare our heights. His goal at that time was to be taller than I was (which was not that hard because I am only 5 feet tall—5'1" if I stretch).

And grow he did! One day, when he was in the beginning of his teens, he hugged me and realized that he had, in fact, outgrown me. "I'm bigger than you!" he said. "You feel like a little bunny!" Later, I told his brothers and sisters what Jud had said. There was an immediate, unanimous decision. "That's right! You are our little bunny and we are all going to take care of you!"

Jud kept growing—or I kept shrinking—because by the time Jud was in high school he was 6 feet tall, 185 lbs., and a wrestler. Still, today, he will hug me up close and say "I'll take care of my little Bunny." I feel so warm and safe.

I am now the Bunny to a sweet little grandson. I look forward to the day when he comes up, grabs me, and measures himself against me to see how tall he is getting. But for now, I think this Bunny will just cuddle this little boy—and hop to do whatever he says!

Cuck

When I was very small, I discovered the cookie jar at my grandmother's house. After sneaking several cookies, my grandmother walked in and caught me. She got on to me so sternly that I started crying.

Wanting to make things right, my grandmother put her hands over her face and started opening and closing them saying "Cuckoo, cuckoo." She was trying her best to make me laugh by acting like a Cuckoo bird! Little did she know that for the next thirty years I would affectionately call her Cuck.

I Love My Grandmother Because...

She is wise.

Granny Holiday

On New Year's, it was resolutions, black-eyed peas for the adults, and horns for the children. Valentine's Day meant cards, candy hearts, and red tablecloths and napkins. On St. Patrick's day, we would wear green or be pinched.

Easter was big! New clothes, church, family lunch, baskets, and egg hunts that would yield clothes, kites, coloring books, and lots and lots of candy.

For the Fourth of July, there was red, white, and blue, and American flags hung everywhere. Halloween brought pumpkins, witches, trick or treat, and candy, candy, and more candy. Thanksgiving involved turkey, dressing with all the trimmings, and rolls—for me it was six rolls with butter and six rolls with gravy! I can still see the dining table with cornucopias and fold-out turkeys and pilgrims from the Hallmark store. And of course the Thanksgiving prayer, recited by my dad.

Birthdays allowed each and every family member to feel special with their own dinner, cake, and many gifts.

But Christmas, Christmas was the one my grandmother planned for all year long. Presents would spill out onto the center of the floor from under the tree. There was food, and goodies that only a picture could illustrate. Red, green, and gold everywhere.

My Granny Holiday made every single holiday a major event for more than forty years.

She died fifteen years ago. For a while I thought I would never view holidays in the same way. But I don't think that's what she would have wanted. I only hope I can make great memories like these for my children and grandchildren.

I Love My Grandmother Because…

She skips all the bad stuff and goes right to the good stuff.

Monging

I was first called Mongingee by my granddaughter because she couldn't pronounce "Grandmommy." Through the years, my name was shortened to Monging. And now that my granddaughter is a sophisticated twenty-two-year-old, I have a much more grown-up name—Mong.

I Love My Grandmother Because...

When I was little, we sat on the bed and watched *Friday the 13th* together!

Grand Ma Ma'

My three daughters, as well as my childhood friends, have consistently teased me about being "dramatic." Thus, when I joyfully learned that my eldest daughter, Brandilin, was to bear our first grandchild, I immediately began asking, "What shall I be called?"

Sorting through a series of ideas, I thought of a dramatic cutting from the play *Anastasia* that I performed in high school. Grand Ma Ma' seemed appropriate.

The beauty, the elation, was hearing it spoken for the first time by sixteen-month-old Virginia. Each time this now precious three-year-old says Grand Ma Ma', there is no doubt the sweetest of names was the proper one for me.

Chuck

My grandmother was a talker. And when she started telling you a story, you knew there would be no interruptions until that story was done! She also loved the old Chuckwagon sandwiches. One of my fondest memories is going over to her house and having a big old roast beef sandwich for lunch.

One day, my grandmother and my aunt were eating out. The waitress did not know that my grandmother had started telling my aunt a story, and she tried to interrupt to get her order.

"I'll have a Chuck and a coke," my grandmother said quickly to the waitress and she continued on with her story.

"I'm sorry, " the waitress said. "Can I have that one more time?"

Exasperated, my grandmother said, "A chuck and a coke."

The poor waitress still did not understand. "I'm sorry, ma'am. I don't understand. Could you tell me one more time?"

Again, my grandmother had to pause from the story. "I said—a chuck and a coke! Oh—oh—I mean a chuckwagon sandwich and a coke." My grandmother's voice changed from aggravated to embarrassed as soon as she realized that she hadn't said the full word "Chuckwagon."

As my aunt repeated this story, she was laughing. "You know Mom. Once she gets on a roll, she doesn't want to be interrupted, not even for a Chuck!"

So we all started calling her Chuck. Of course this led to other names like Chuckmeister and Chuckaroo. She was the greatest.

I Love My Grandmother Because…

She always says, "What do you want to do today?"
and then we do whatever I want to do!

Choo Choo

Our immediate family lived in Tennessee, and our aunts, uncles, and cousins lived in Ohio. When my brother and I were little, we would make many visits to Ohio with our grandmother. We would travel to Ohio via train. We were two little boys living every little boy's dream! A trip on a choo-choo train! As the train slowly began to move, the whistle would blow and the choo-choo sound would begin. We would snuggle in close to our grandmother, Choo Choo, feeling safe and secure. Excitement filled our stomachs and adventure filled our minds.

Choo Choo is ninety years old now. Although train trips are not the norm anymore, just the thought of Choo Choo stirs wonderful memories of the excitement of our trips and the fun we had visiting our extended family in Ohio.

GaGa

*I*could not decide on a grandmother name. To be honest, I was feeling a little sorry for myself that I was even at the age where I could become a grandmother.

One day, as I sat thumbing through a magazine, there—miraculously—appeared an article about a grandmother who would ride motorcycles, climb mountains, parachute, and even bungee jump. Automatically I was revitalized!

Her name was GaGa, so I decided that that would be a great name for me. It personified energy, fun and youthfulness. My grandchildren call me GaGa today, and believe me we do many fun and exciting things together. I have not—by the way—ever bungee jumped. I may have energy—but I'm not crazy!

Granny Girl

*S*he was a very young mother of an older daughter and a younger nine-year-old stepdaughter. All of the "girls," as her stepdaughter would say, loved to spend time together. She would play games with them, take them to amusement parks to ride the roller coasters, and talk with them into the wee hours of the night.

When her older daughter announced that she was going to be a mother, the younger daughter protested, "You are too young to be a grandmother! I think the baby should call you Granny Girl!"

And so she was Granny Girl from then on, young at heart and full of fun.

I Love My Grandmother Because...

She buys me stuff—and I mean good stuff, like Slurpies and candy!

Nana Hub

When my husband and I entered our marriage, it was the second for both of us. With our combined families, we had four children. One of the biggest dilemmas that we found ourselves in was that both my husband's mother and my mother were called Nana.

Therefore, we decided to include an extension to their Nana names. My mother was called Nana Roy, because her last name was Pomeroy and it was easy to shorten. Because my husband's mother loved nursery rhymes, we decided to name her Nana Hub, short for Old Mother Hubbard. Of course hub also means heart, core, center—and that's what Nana Hub had been to my husband's family for many years.

The truth is, at the hub of our family, we have two very special Nanas.

Kozo

*M*y name is Agnes Kozjack White. When I was in high school, my chemistry teacher dubbed me Kozo. People have called me that since that time. I love to paint watercolors—all sorts of pictures, including landscapes and clowns. When my grandchildren were young, they would try to call me Kozo, but it would come out Koco. My youngest grandchild still calls me Koco, but as the others grew, they changed to Kozo. I am very happy and proud to answer to either name.

I Love My Grandmother Because...

Every Sunday she took me to buy ice cream!

I Love My Grandmother Because…

She is very funny and makes me laugh!

—

She taught me to keep scrapbooks.

—

She was a great storyteller.

—

She taught me to fold napkins and set the table.

—

She plays ball with me.

—

She washed my face with a soft cloth and Woodbury soap.

Bum Mother

When they were small, the twins Mike and Lynne had difficulty saying "Grandmother." Their version for referring to their paternal grandmother came out as "Bum Mother." Bum Mother died when they were still young children, so Mike and Lynne never made the transition to "Grandmother." They still remember her fondly when snuggling under the many quilts she made. One friendship quilt is especially cherished because it includes Bum Mother's initials and those of many other relatives, neighbors, and friends from the rural West Tennessee community where she lived.

One generation passeth away, and another generation cometh.
—ECCLESIASTES 1:4

Great Ways to Help Your Grandchild Remember You

1. Have a special story that you read to him or her.

2. Make a tape recording of special memories of your family history, of their parents' experiences, or of your feelings the first time that you held them.

3. Find out what their favorite food is and always have that available to them whenever they are at your house.

4. Sing a special song to them each time they are around.

5. Videotape yourself reading a book, telling funny stories, or even talking about your family history.

6. Develop a special code—whether it be a look, a pat, or a phrase that is special between only the two of you.

7. Start a tradition with them that is special only to them. For instance, send them a special flower on their birthday every year.

Boo-Boo Nana

His earliest recollection of his grandmother was with a broken arm. In fact, it seemed to him that his grandmother always had some sort of boo-boo. Both he and his grandmother found it extremely funny that every time he saw her she had had another sort of accident. When his parents would say they were going to Nana's, he would call out, "Are we going to Boo-Boo Nana's?" This was how he could distinguish the two grandmothers in his life.

She dearly took to the name of Boo-Boo Nana and not accidentally, she is called that to this day by all of her grandchildren.

I Love My Grandmother Because...

She loves me.

Grammie

One Halloween night, I opened the door to the most adorable little three- or four-year-old spook. He asked me if I had any children. I told him, "I have big children, but my daughter will soon be having a little baby."

On hearing my good news, this precious little child dropped his bag of treats, put both hands to his face, looked at me with big eyes filled with more love than you can imagine, and exclaimed, "You're going to be a Grammie?"

I knew then I wanted to be called Grammie. I also wanted to be the kind of Grammie who would create the kind of love I saw in that child's eyes.

I am Grammie now. I don't know who the little spook was, but I do know there is another Grammie out there who has done something right to cause such excitement in her small grandchild's voice with the very mention of the word "Grammie."

Mamie

When I was born, my Mamie, who lived with us, was in her fifties. She was full of life and could be found most any time dancing around our house. Mamie was a comforter, encourager—my biggest fan. On top of that, she embodied every definition of the word "grandmother"—and more.

She was a retired schoolteacher; every night when I got home from school, she would study with me. Once when we were conjugating Latin verbs—and I was sick and tired of doing it—I pitched a little fit and stormed out of the room.

Later, feeling guilty about how I had behaved, I walked back into her room to apologize.

"David," she said to me, "you never need to apologize to me for anything. I know you would never do or say anything intentionally to hurt me."

At that moment, I knew the meaning of unconditional love. She had that for me, and I for her. Isn't that a beautiful sign of a grandmother?